Cover image: *The Architects*, RB Kitaj, 1981, private collection.

KITAJ: THE ARCHITECTS
COLIN ST JOHN WILSON AND MJ LONG

black dog
publishing
london uk

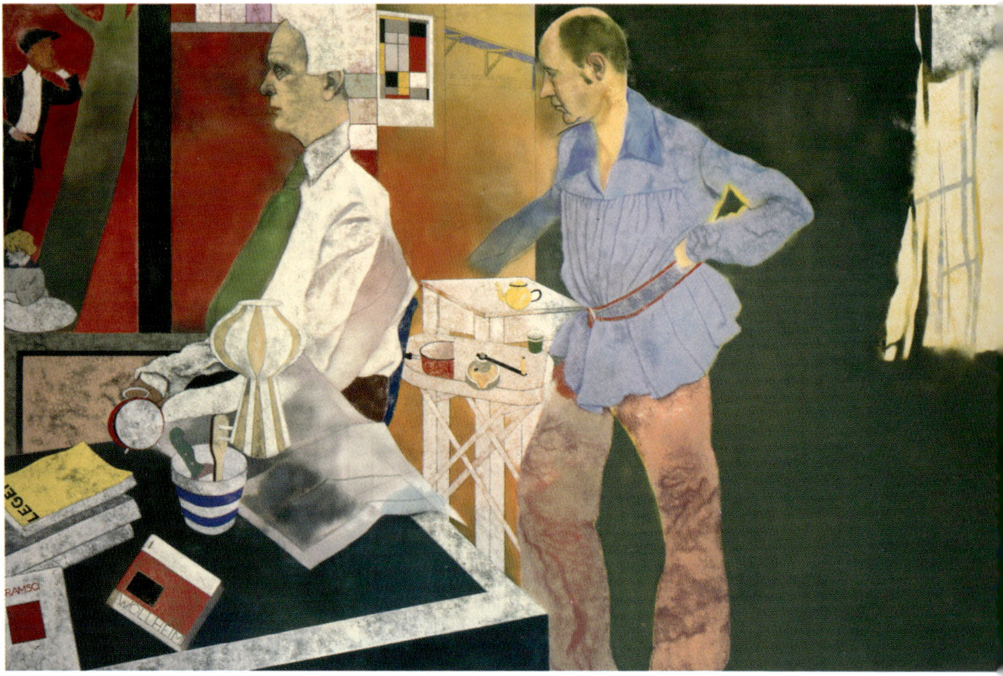

Above: *From London: James Joll and John Golding*, RB Kitaj, 1975–1976, private collection.
Overleaf left: Rear facade, Kitaj's remodelled studio.
Overleaf right: MJ Long and RB Kitaj discussing plans, 1974.

INTRODUCTION

SANDY. To celebrate the remodelling (by my wife) of his house in Elm Park Road, Kitaj resolved to make a portrait of us—in the first instance as tall separate full size monochromatic oil paintings, and later a single family group to include our children—Sarah and Harry.

The execution of this work was largely carried out by the artist in solitude, unlike the two paintings that form the 'case studies' in my book *The Artist at Work*.

It was an important time in Kitaj's development, when he was beginning to re-shape his whole working method and quite certainly the result was nothing like *If not, not* and the double portrait *From London: James Joll and John Golding* that he had recently completed—and which was the kind of thing that I had hoped for! There was the exciting, disturbing awareness that we were guinea-pigs in an experimental operation to renew the artist's visionary powers. The talk circled around propositions of something "entirely new" and "important", but finally settled for what "I guess you'd call a transitional work...."

The ambiguous "collage" space and impeccable surface textures of the Joll/Golding painting are replaced by unitary space, direct painting from life , and a rich gestural handling of thick paint built up in layers of scumbling. As with all Kitaj's work, the image contains associations and allusions: the quality of light and the key to the colour scheme are both drawn from the van Gogh *The Night Café* which is in the collection at Yale—to which reference is also made in MJ's Yale sweatshirt. My own notes contain references to periods of intensely concentrated drawing, both in pencil studies and directly onto the canvas.

Most of the toil in developing the picture compositionally and technically was fought out in later stages and in solitude.

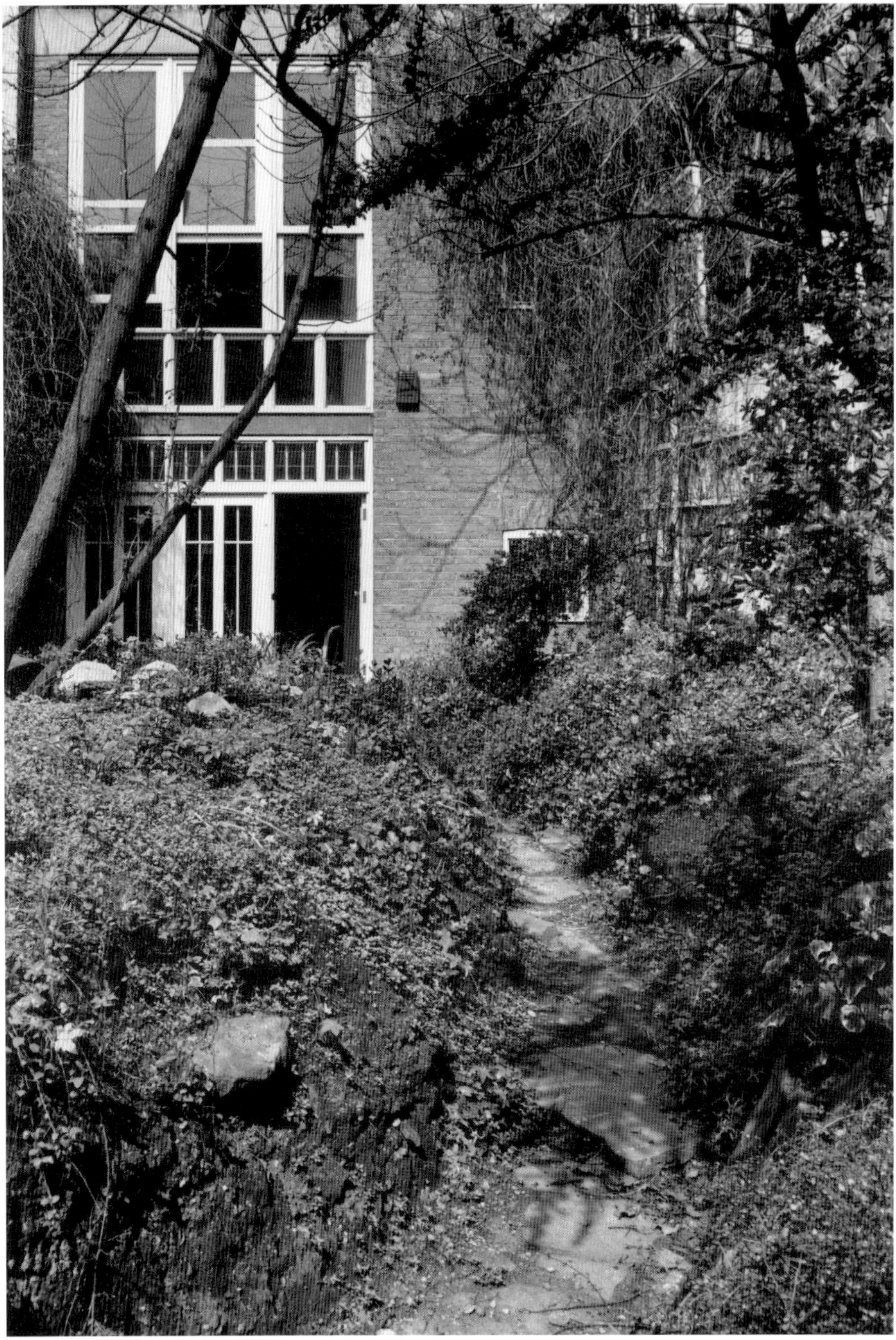

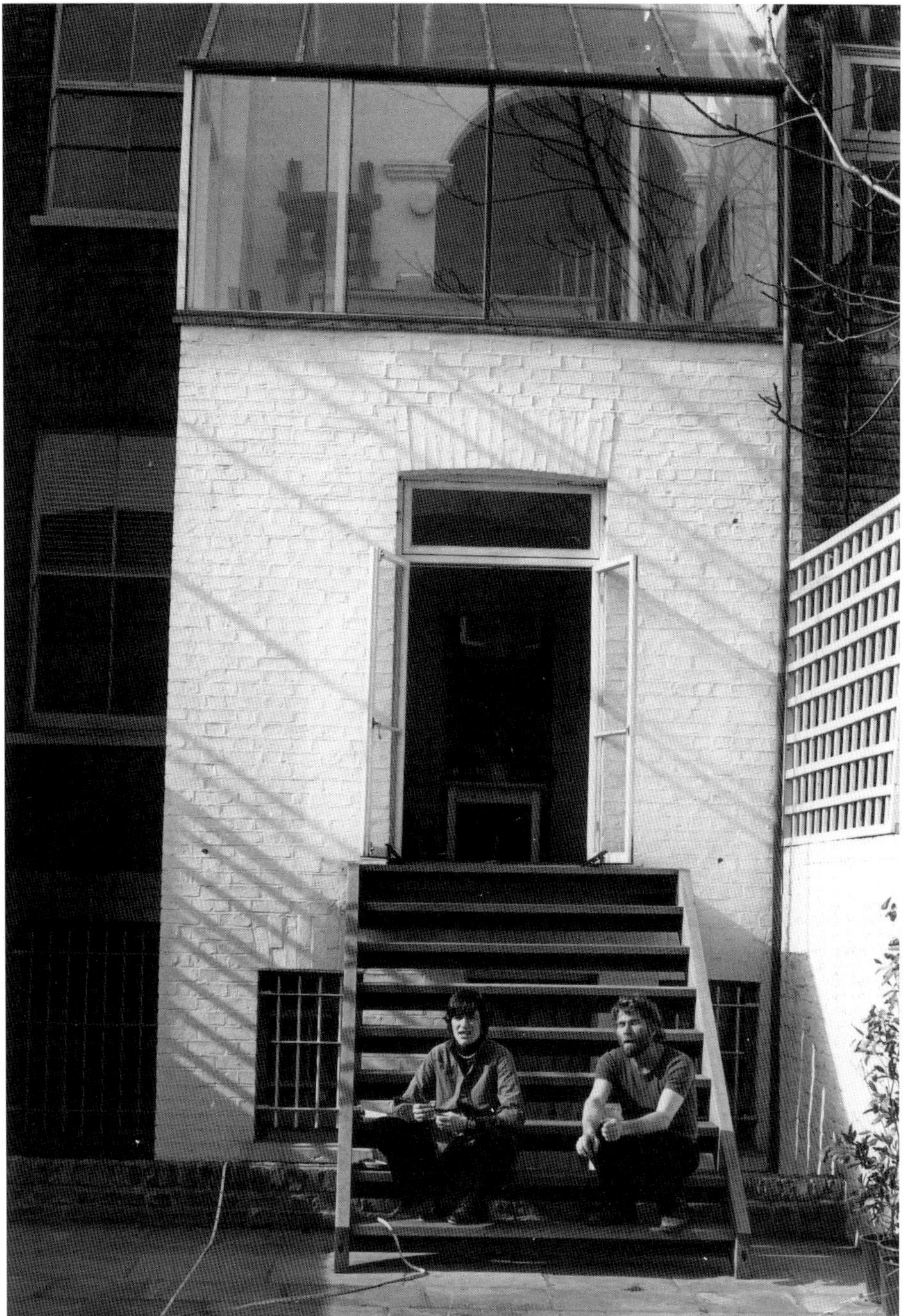

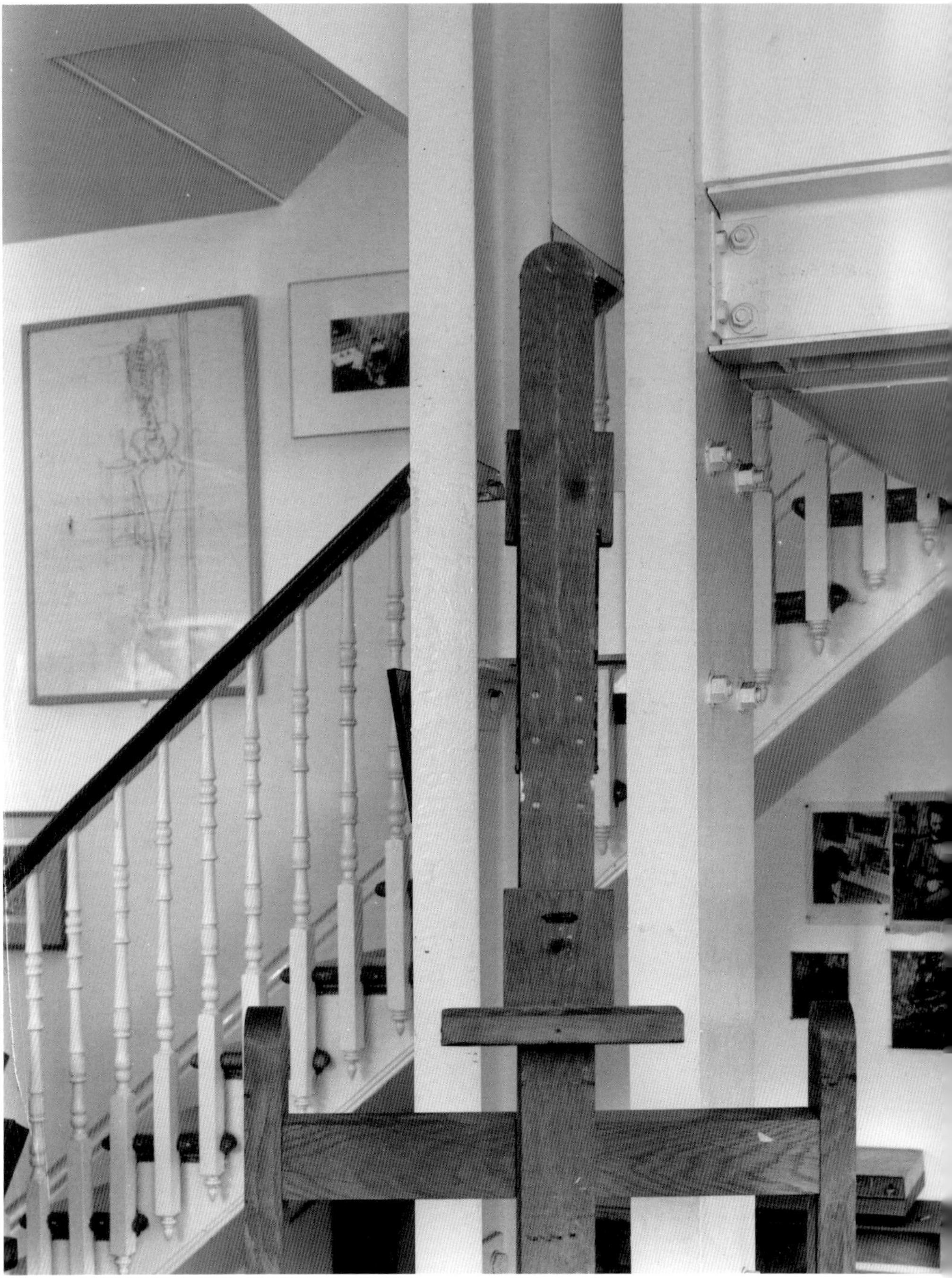

SITTING SCHEDULE

Sittings started early in August 1979. The first notes are dated 19 September and refer to earlier sittings.

1979

19 SEPTEMBER	MJ
20 SEPTEMBER	SANDY
5 OCTOBER	MJ
13 OCTOBER	SANDY
27 OCTOBER	SANDY
19 DECEMBER	SANDY
26 DECEMBER	MJ

1980

JANUARY	MJ
1 FEBRUARY	MJ
10 FEBRUARY	MJ
23 FEBRUARY	SANDY
26 APRIL	SANDY
7 JUNE	SANDY

1981

19 FEBRUARY	SANDY
27 NOVEMBER	PAINTING DELIVERED

Opposite: Kitaj studio, with the steel structure supporting the house above.

19 SEPTEMBER 1979 (AND BEFORE)

MJ. I should have started this when RB first began on our portraits. But I'll see if I can remember what he's done so far. At first, he talked about two separate portraits—black and white; tall and thin. Sandy finally diffidently asked whether we could be together—more of a painting (like Duncan and Creeley) and RB was enthusiastic.

About six weeks ago, he did a sketching session (about an hour and a half) with each of us. Heads only in "characteristic" poses (all very self-conscious this, for me). He started describing a look of mine that I think has to do with listening intently (about to pounce, maybe). I said (v. embarrassed) he'd just have to put my head where he wanted it. So he did—slightly tilted and turned a little away. He sketched and photographed and got enthusiastic about the Yale shirt. He did the same for Sandy—in his case the "look" was over the top of his glasses.

Then, I suppose about a month ago, he decided to set us up in front of his new stepped bookcase and to do a sort of Seurat 'machine' as a vehicle for the portrait. So more photographs—me walking (standing) away to the left and looking back.

Then about 12 September, RB decided he'd like the children in the background, so we went over and he photographed Sarah Jane and Harry (smoking his pipe) in the middle of the floor. And there was the canvas with some line drawings of us all in front of the bookcase, with my face in tone, looking (I thought) like me, but RB wasn't satisfied—sat me next to it and said the proportions were wrong.

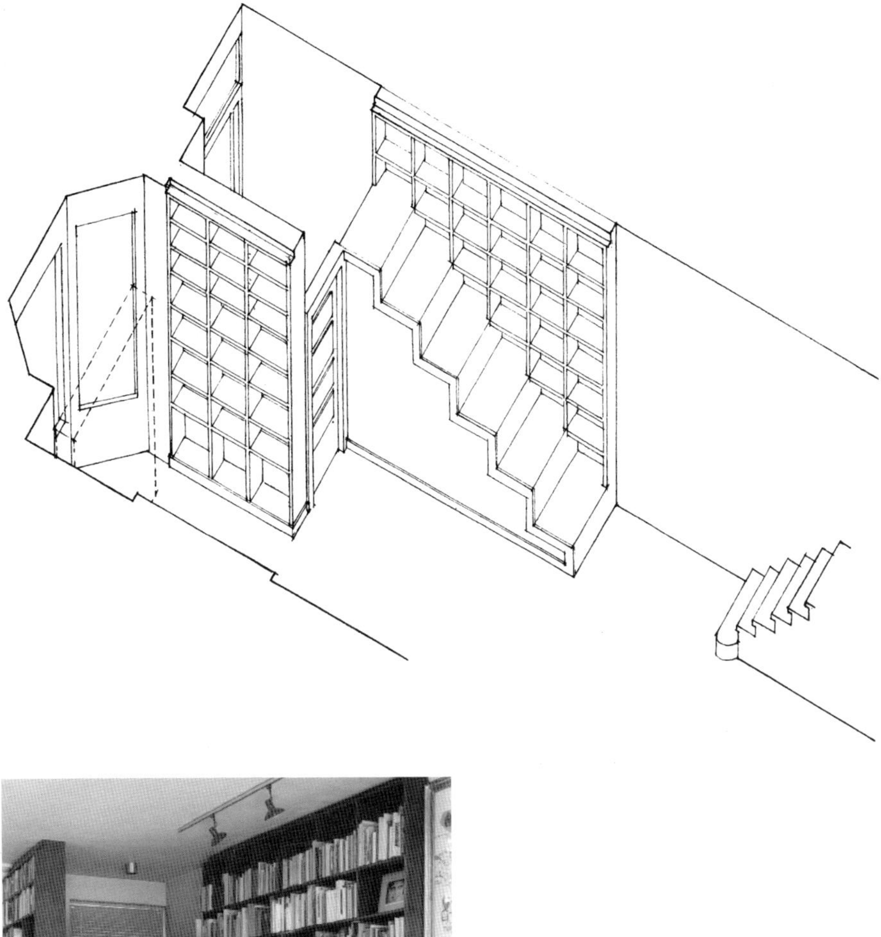

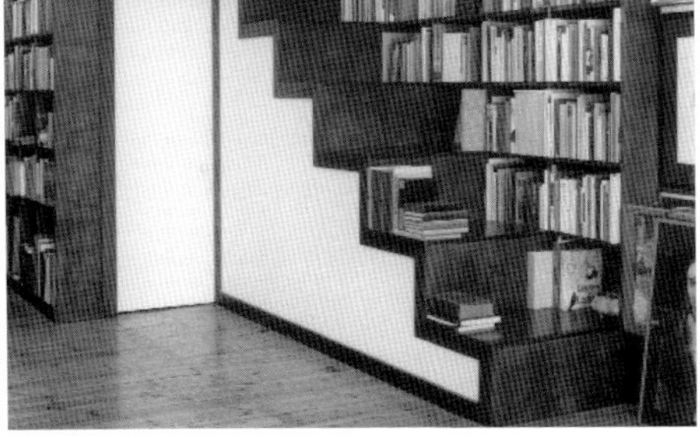

Top: Sketch of entry and stepped bookcase, MJ Long.
Bottom: Photograph of completed bookcase.

(19 SEPTEMBER)

This time I sat to the side of the canvas, and he drew straight on it in charcoal.

The light was coming from my right rather than the left (as in the first sketch). Doesn't that matter?

The kids were gone from the canvas—he said he thought they might just be emergent smudges.

He drew for about an hour, then stood back and said it was all wrong. So he attacked it with solvent and a rag. This evidently takes the solvent off as well. I asked why he drew in tone rather than just line. He said that he didn't really set out to do a tone drawing, but that he seemed to be able to control it better that way.

He then started drawing again. There's no talking during all this—I get quite hypnotised with the whole thing, and feel as if I could draw his eyes quite accurately—particularly his right eye. He finally said—"I'm getting lost in this. Good. I'm drawing very slowly."

At the end he said that it was an interesting drawing but not such a good portrait. It looked a great drawing to me. He said he'd widened the upper part of the face (the part he'd been working on). He said that was his instinct—especially with the wide bookcase shelf behind. The opposite of Giacometti's instinct, he said—broadening the face was like mapping the features—laying them out.

The colours will be the sort of red, green, and yellow that van Gogh used in *The Night Café*. And incidentally, the composition is similar—long floor and a little ceiling and a door in roughly the same place. RBK isn't sure which came first—the colour intentions or the realisation that the compositions are related. RBK says he's not like Auerbach—doesn't erase the whole lot when something doesn't work. RBK takes out the offending bit—Auerbach apparently scrubs the whole thing out at the beginning of each section—over and over again.

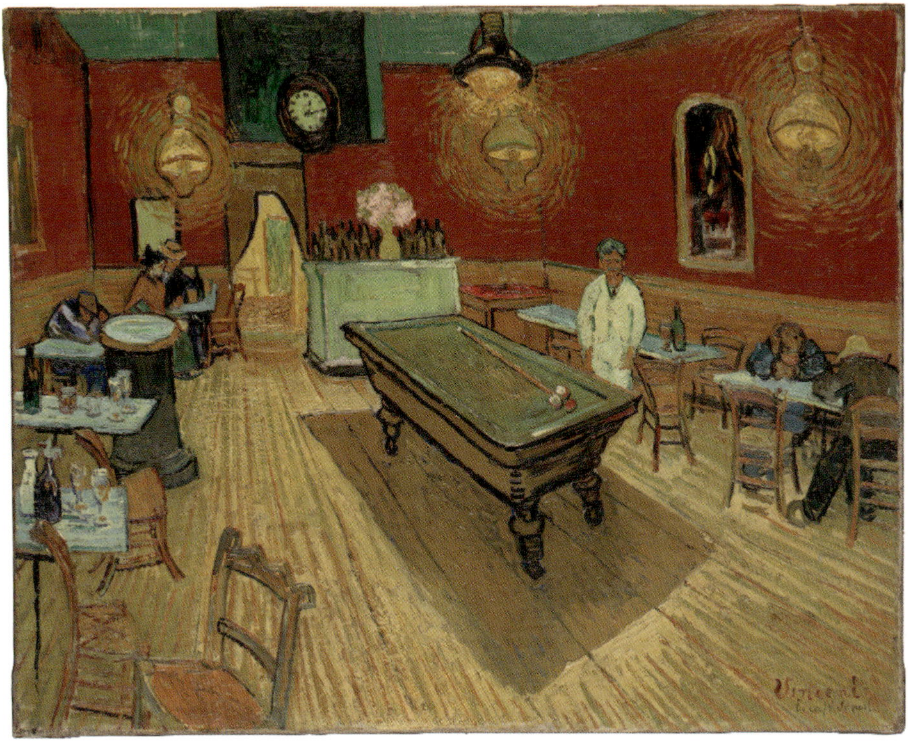

Le Café de Nuit (*The Night Café*), Vincent van Gogh, 1888.

20 SEPTEMBER 1979

SANDY. RBK has altered MJ's right eye and didn't like his revision: otherwise the head looked fine. Me vague outlines only: background architecture strongly drawn. One red patch on top riser of bookcase.

Title is to be "The Architects" (cf "the Ambassadors").

He then talked about the van Gogh, the flukey similarities in composition.

He then asked me to pose for hands—to be grouped in between left corner of painting: so I sat at the round table with a kelim on it. Many photographs. Then as I leant to my left he suddenly concentrated on revising the pose that way—me to be swayed across the composition, MJ vertical and steady, SJ between us, and Harry on extreme left of the picture—but the kids only adumbrated.

Considered that my tie would be helpful compositionally. Then he drew directly on the canvas—overall pose and then concentrating on the head. The sun falling onto the half of the canvas from behind him projected his drawing as a shadow play onto the surface which I could follow. He talked well about (Walter) Benjamin, central for him and now distressingly fashionable. No talk while drawing head. More photography of head (glasses keep slipping down slightly) and overall pose. About an hour and a half's work in all.

He said I was coming out as a cross between Jean-Paul Sartre and Stanley Spencer.

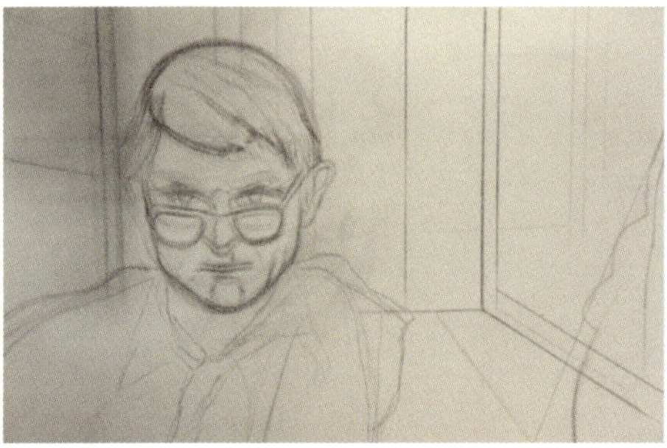

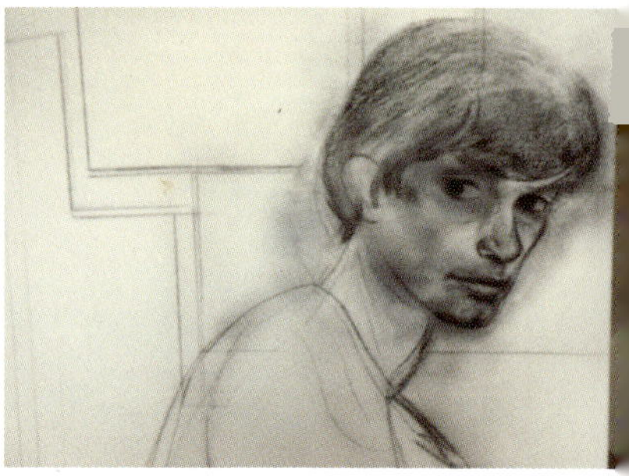

Above and opposite: Photographs of work in progress, RB Kitaj.

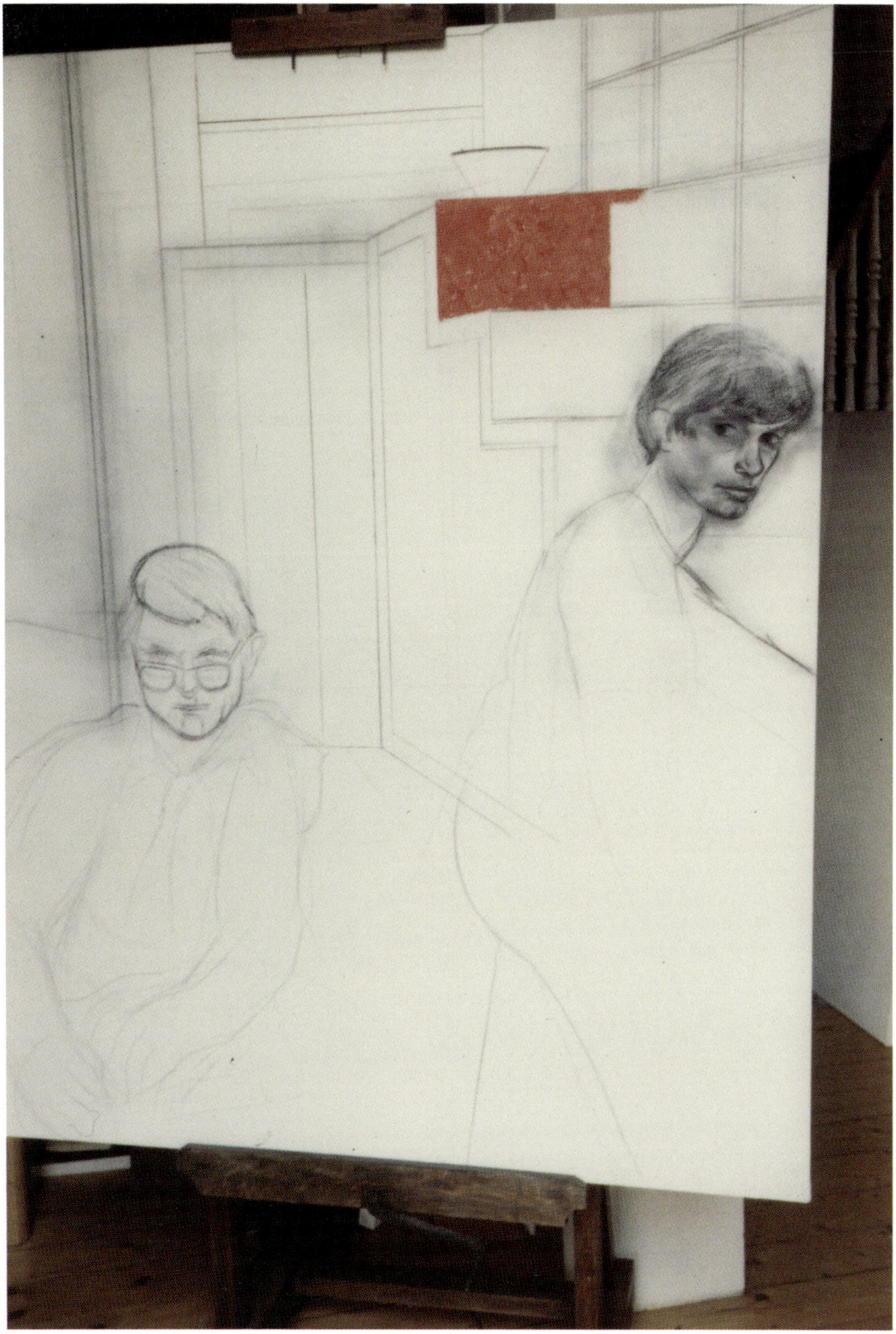

5 OCTOBER 1979

MJ. I went for a short session. RB produced his first set of photos.

He has now laid in some green, some blue in the window over the door, and some more red to the left of the door. Not, thank goodness, so far too much of the more bilious greeny yellowy of the van Gogh. The colour is put on splodgy and with relief brush strokes—disconcerting if you are expecting his usual dry flatness. He said he wants the coloured areas to be much more varied now, and he intends to use some of the techniques of the Impressionists. The blobby plain colours will shine through more delicate layers on top. The present set of paintings (40 in all) is the first on which he's tried this.

He has also drawn in SJ from one of the photos—a coy SJ hovering in the door—big oval forehead under her hair band. He said the photos of Harry were not so good and took one that I had with me, taken when Mana was here, showing Harry and his 'bed' doing a sort of war dance in the middle of the floor.

He did some drawing, saying that the mouth and chin were good but the eyes were wrong. We talked more at the beginning. He said "I'm chisling at it like a piece of sculpture." He said he much preferred working from people than photos—we're the third lot—Duncan and Creeley, James Kirkman, and us.

He said that with his new painting technique, he intended to draw more with the paint.

He showed me his last photos of Sandy and was excited by the sun on his hands in the foreground. He might do sort of spotlit hands in the corner and is convinced about the Kelim pattern, the blue shirt, and the rumpled tie.

At the end of drawing, he said it had gone nowhere, and I must say it looked a bit that way to me.

We were talking about his graphics (because we have so much up post burglary), and he said that he was only beginning to look at all that stuff again—he was rather ashamed of himself for joining the glossy silk-screen collage thing. He won't have another print show until he has lots of real etchings and lithographs to balance the other stuff.

13 OCTOBER 1979 (SATURDAY)

SANDY. MJ off to Yale, Mrs Bennett with children, I to RBK (met over snack lunch at 'BJ' 1:30).

RBK dissatisfied with MJ's head—he certainly seems to have the jaw a bit heavy and to have muffed the right eye a little. Sarah Jane rather Balthus-like.

He concentrated on drawing (no photos at all) reworking my glasses and mouth: then after a break, the eyes. Very intensive—almost two hours in all. He was very satisfied with the work—me too: said he was now ready to start painting my head, that it had now overtaken MJ's. He intended to concentrate during December on the painting.

We talked about collectors (I am one of about three that he knows whose interest is a genuine passion for the work; actually that may be true—I can't even understand how the dealer can let go of a picture that seems to me to be magical) and about dealers—who count among their number four of the five people he most dislikes...!

Much of the time I could not talk—when he was working on the mouth: when he worked on the eyes they got very sore with unfocussed staring. RBK spoke of the need to give the heads psychological depth—Munch, early Kokoschka, Freud, and of course Rembrandt and all the old masters.

RBK "In one sense you can see that everything that Picasso ad Matisse did was a kind of logical step from a given starting point: but where on earth Cézanne and van Gogh got the vision of their world is unfathomable; crazy."

He also made a distinction between the modes of Matisse, that he found more "expressive", and of Giacometti, that he found more objective and analytical. Cézanne midway. (Check back on this argument).

27 OCTOBER 1979

SANDY. Saturday. RBK gave me a cold beef salad lunch.

Kitaj had covered a lot more canvas with a heavy impasto. (Central area, surrounding S Jane and stair.) I was surprised that he proceeded to paint my head directly. There seemed to me to be something rather self-conscious about the variety of types of brush stroke, hand positions for holding the brush, etc.. I wondered if this was some reflection on his earlier comment that Bomberg was so much more original in conception, range, and even painterly touch than either Auerbach or Kossoff. It emerged that this way of painting was for him entirely new—"I hope it comes off, but in any case I promise you it will finally be smoothed down a lot...".

One bit of telepathy. I was thinking about his Golding/Joll painting and wondering if there was any significance in the fact that we were posed to look straight back at him (obviously not, since many of his recent 'portraits' do just that) and assuming that that had certainly not been painted from the model, when he said "this is the first time I have painted directly from the model since the Golding and Joll painting".

He scumbled in the shirt. RBK on the whole very satisfied with it and hopes it is going to be very strong. Two hours work. Very intense.

Opposite: Photograph of work in progress, RB Kitaj.

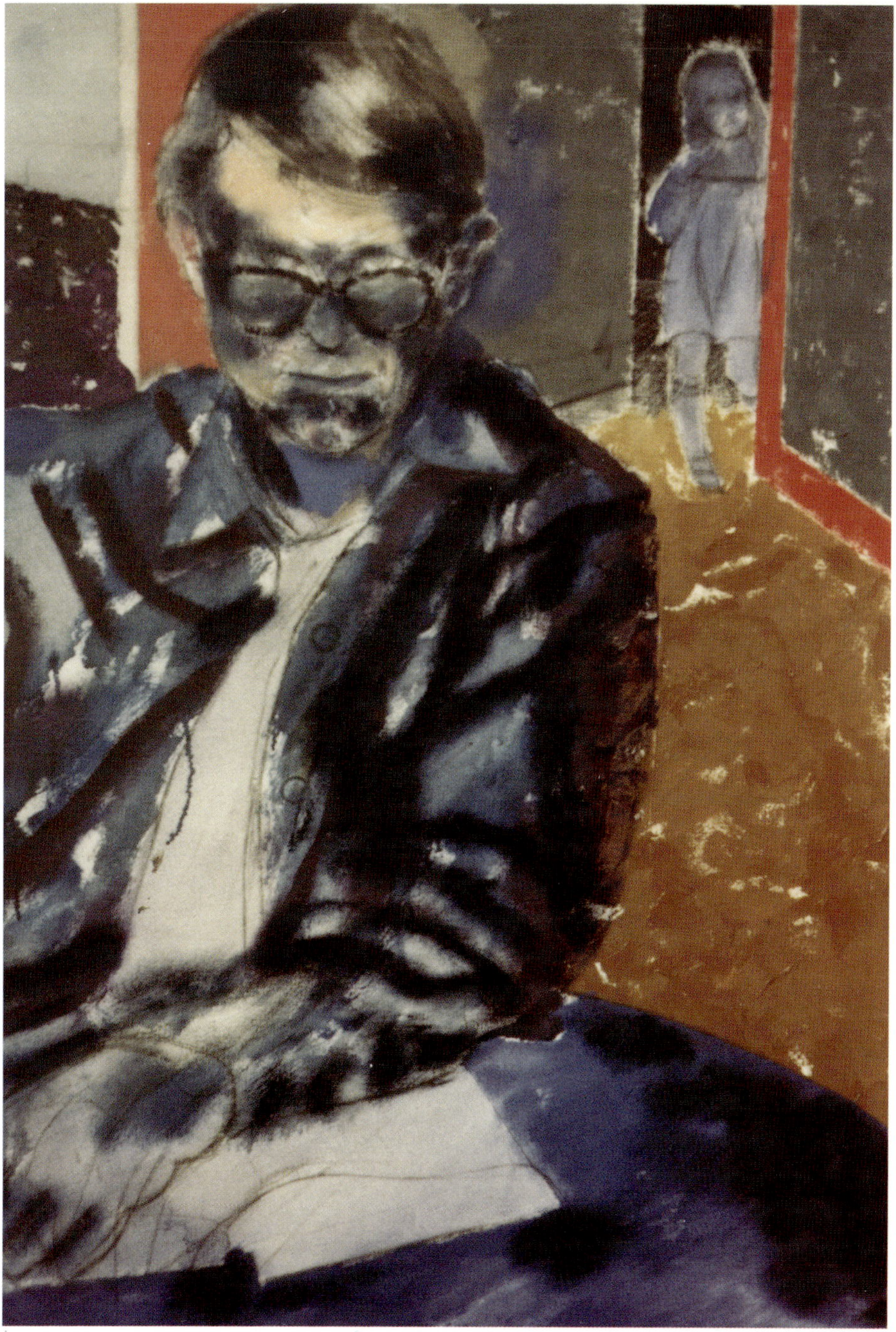

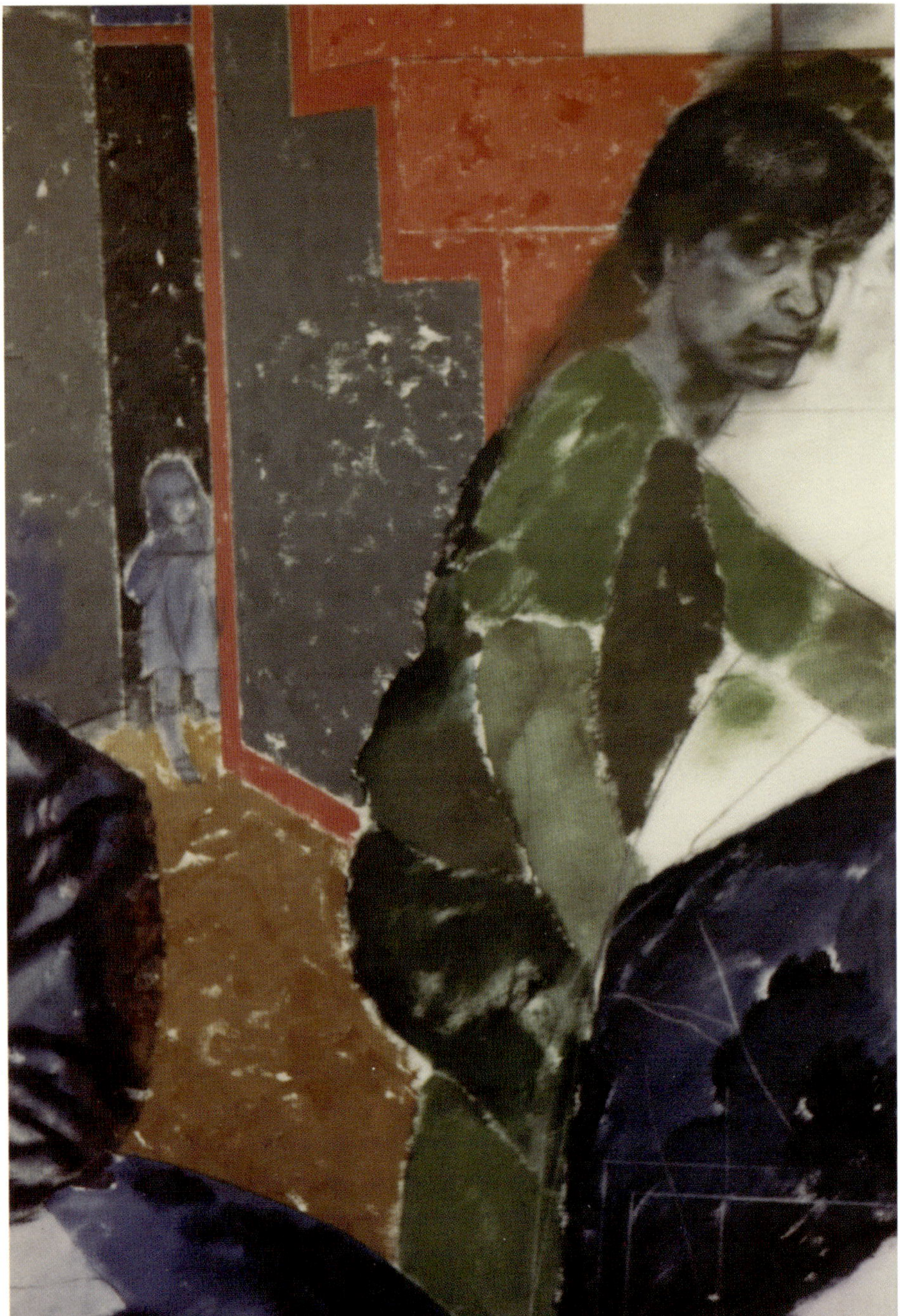

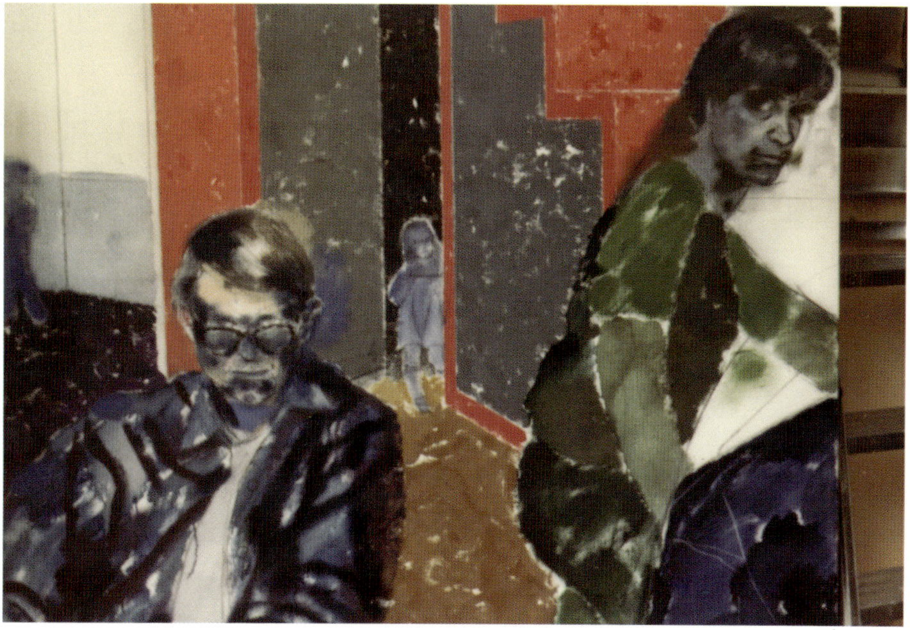

Opposite and above: Photographs of work in progress, RB Kitaj.

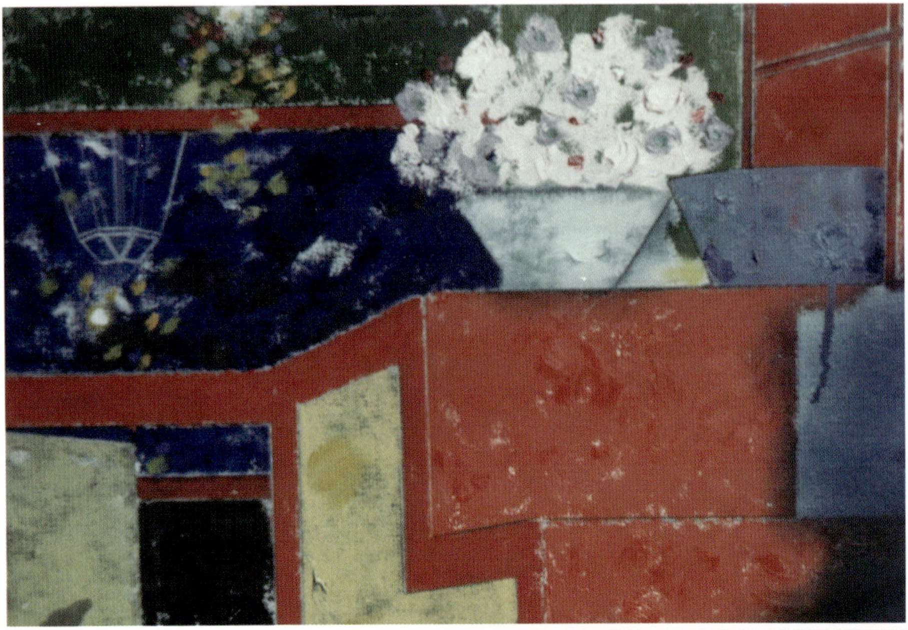

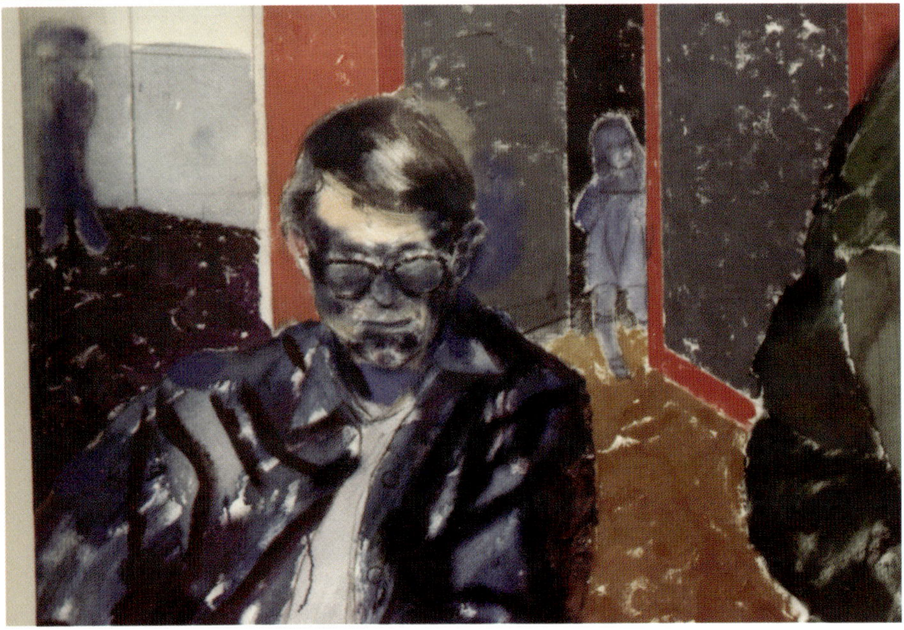

Top and bottom: Photographs of work in progress, RB Kitaj.

19 DECEMBER 1979 (WEDNESDAY)

SANDY. Since the last sitting, a great deal of work has been done on the overall composition—in fact the whole canvas is now massed in, albeit that much is an underlay. Mostly thick pigment with evident brush strokes. RB is very pleased with the composition, it will be an important painting still retaining certain hints from the van Gogh. There is a lamp located in the porch which may be some reference: also the red of the bookcase details relates to the wall colour in the van Gogh.

I suggested he make it a mirror and put himself in: Velázquez.

But both figures have been scumbled over with a dark blue tone. The painting framing my head has been causing a lot of trouble because it looks too much like an abstract. (The vertical bearing down on my head reminds me of a Mantegna, but I didn't mention it.)

RB worked for about an hour and a half on my face using a French stippling pencil called? (wound up blotting paper brought to a point—sharpenable) which he dabbed periodically into black/blue? paint which he had scooped onto a palette knife which he held almost vertically in his left hand. He said it was the tool used by David Hockney for his early figure drawings at the College, dipping into charcoal and linseed: he had used it to do the portraits of David, Robert Duncan and La Passionaria. At the end of the session he had done little more than re-draw the glasses.

I said it was a pity to turn MJ's head into pure profile as he had suggested to her that he might try. His reply was that he thought it rather too obvious to have both faces staring straight back at the beholder—so I suggested that he should lower my eyes (which I would prefer anyway—more 'quietist').

RB is now working full-time on the painting and hopes to get the 'composition' finished by the New Year even if the heads still have to be worked on a lot.

26 DECEMBER 1979

MJ. Probably not a great deal more done since Sandy's last session. The street light is both a reference to van Gogh and an excuse for the kind of glowing light he wants to produce in the background. The children are both in now—very dark—cobalt underpainting—they won't stay that way. Sarah Jane's legs have gone rather pudgy in the process. Harry is in contemplative "smoking" mood. A lot more work has been done to Sandy's left eye, forehead and cheek. The rough painting is based directly on the Monet Cathedrals with (for example) bright red showing through an oatmealy layer. Further splodges of colour will relate areas more to each other. RB says he has to be careful not to get the under layers too thick or the paint will crack. He says this will be the basis of a whole group of paintings for which it will act as a 'teaching' painting. He said that he would like to keep the painting around for a longer period and that he always rather regrets letting one go to the Marlborough.

He worked with cobalt from the tube on the compressed paper stylus. (He says the usual stuff would be charcoal and linseed oil.) He worked on the same old 3/4 view (very hard to hold without watering eyes with the sun streaming in behind his head). With the (now familiar) complete dissatisfaction at the end. Apparently the structural relationships are wrong. I said that if he really wanted to draw me in profile, he should go ahead and do it.

Anyhow, I left feeling obscurely guilty for the lack of success with RB grumpy and abstracted.

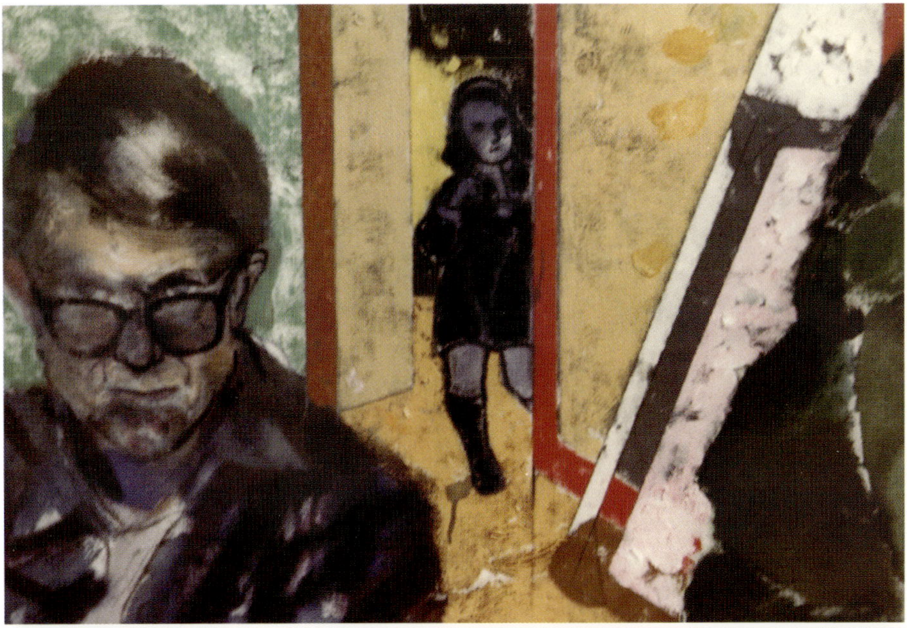

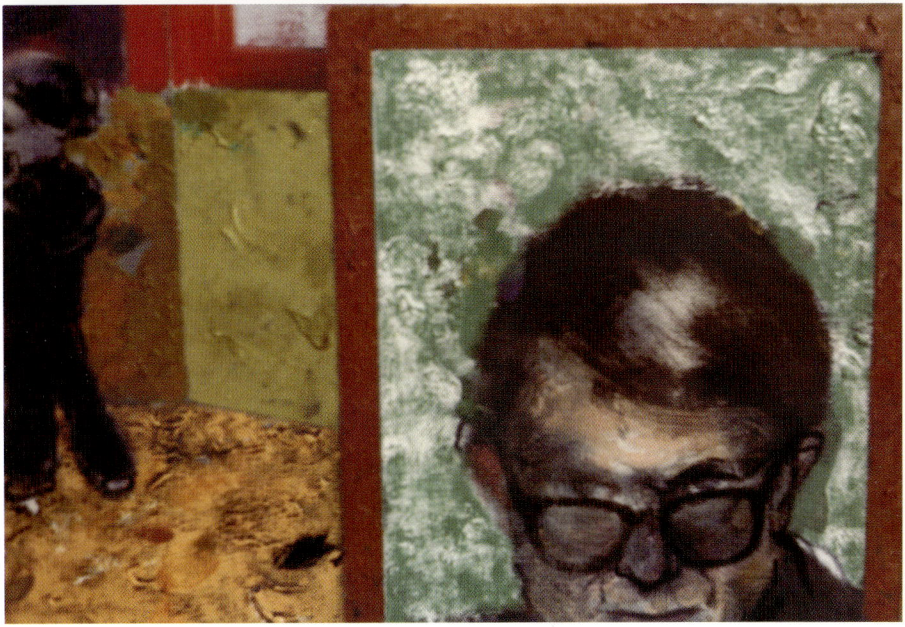

Top and bottom: Photographs of work in progress, RB Kitaj.

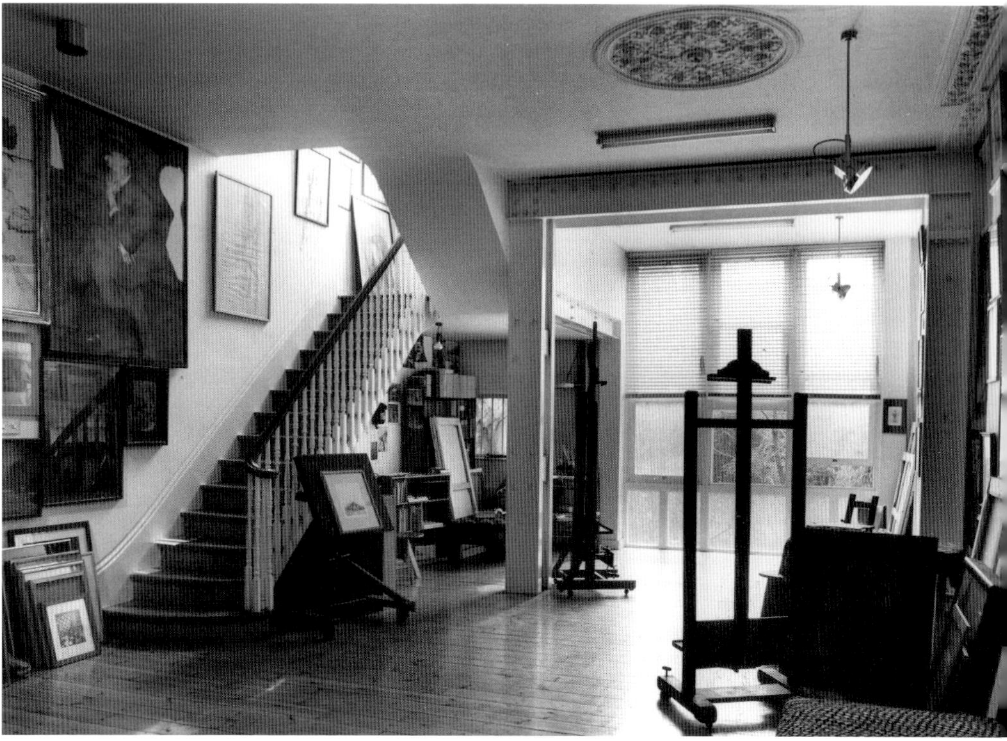

Above and opposite: Kitaj studio.

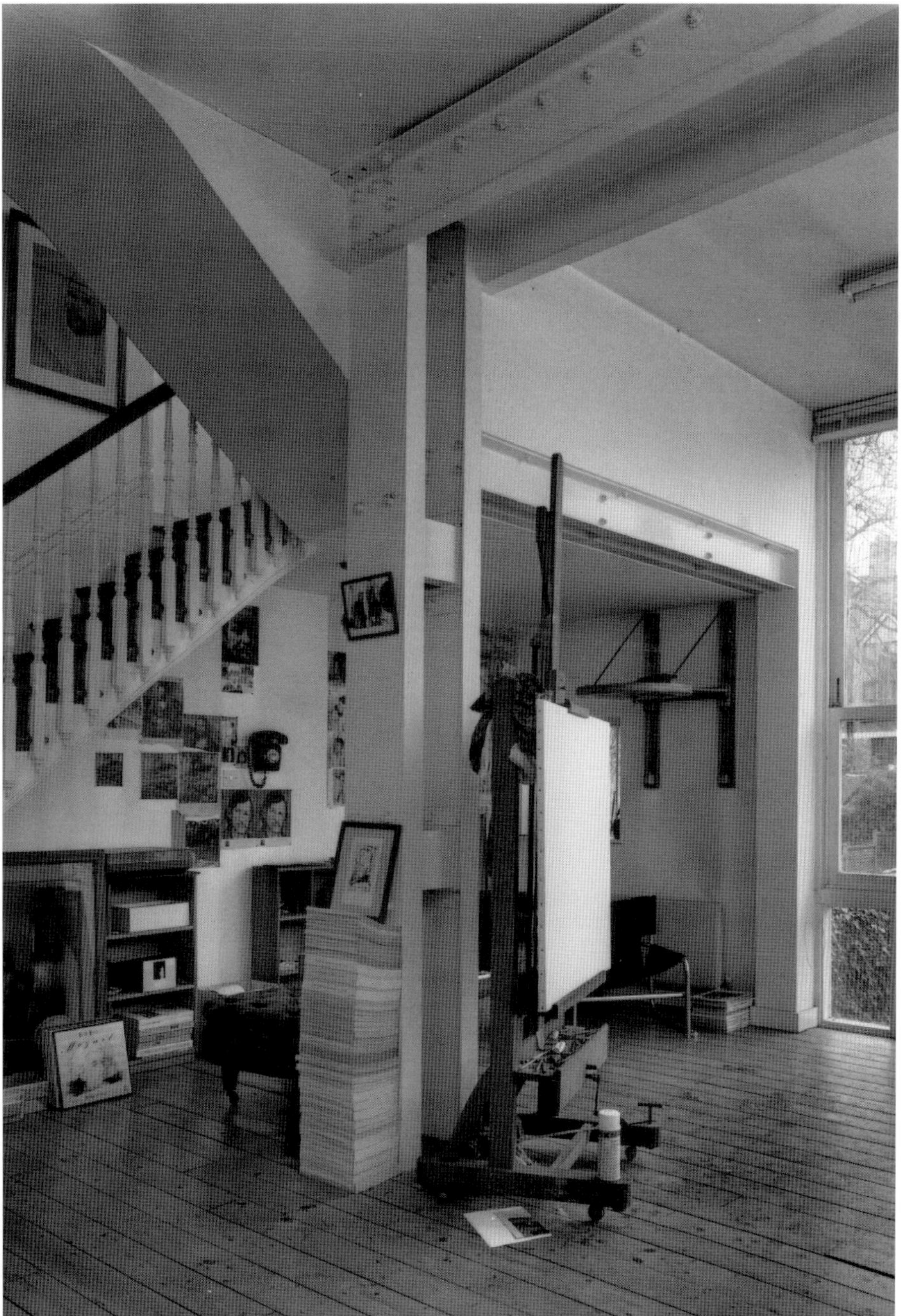

JANUARY 1980
A CONVERSATION.

MJ. At the British Museum Restaurant:

I said that I came away feeling guilty about the struggle he seemed to be having with my face. He said nonsense—we all have the sense that anything that's really good comes out of some kind of struggle.

He said he thinks it's one of his most important paintings—a change of direction. It will be in a show in October.* He seems to think most people think he's making a mistake.

*note: at the Marlborough. There were to have been ten oil paintings, but now there will only be ours plus pastels. (Later note by S.)

Opposite: Kitaj at work in his studio surrounded by his 'filing system'.

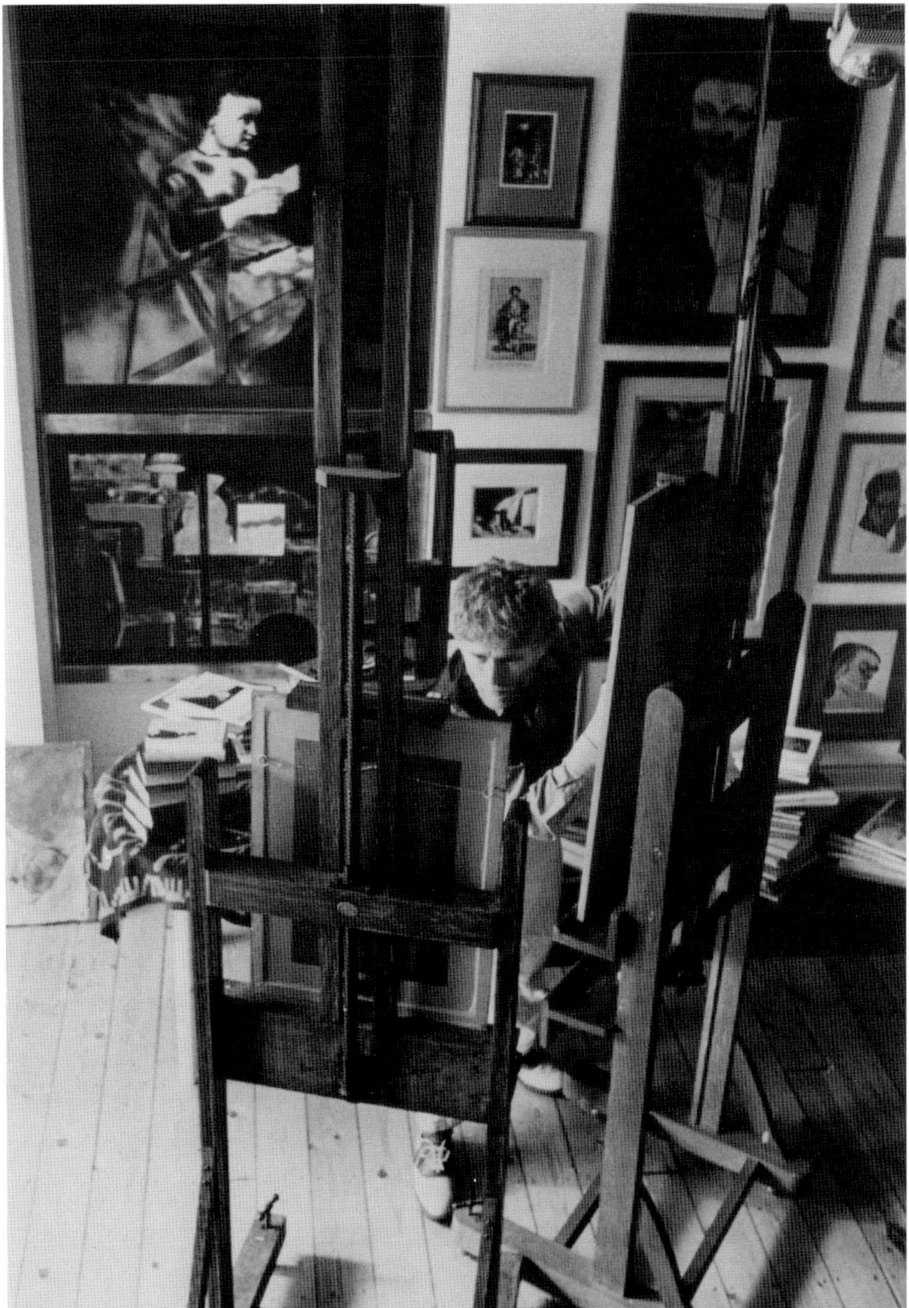

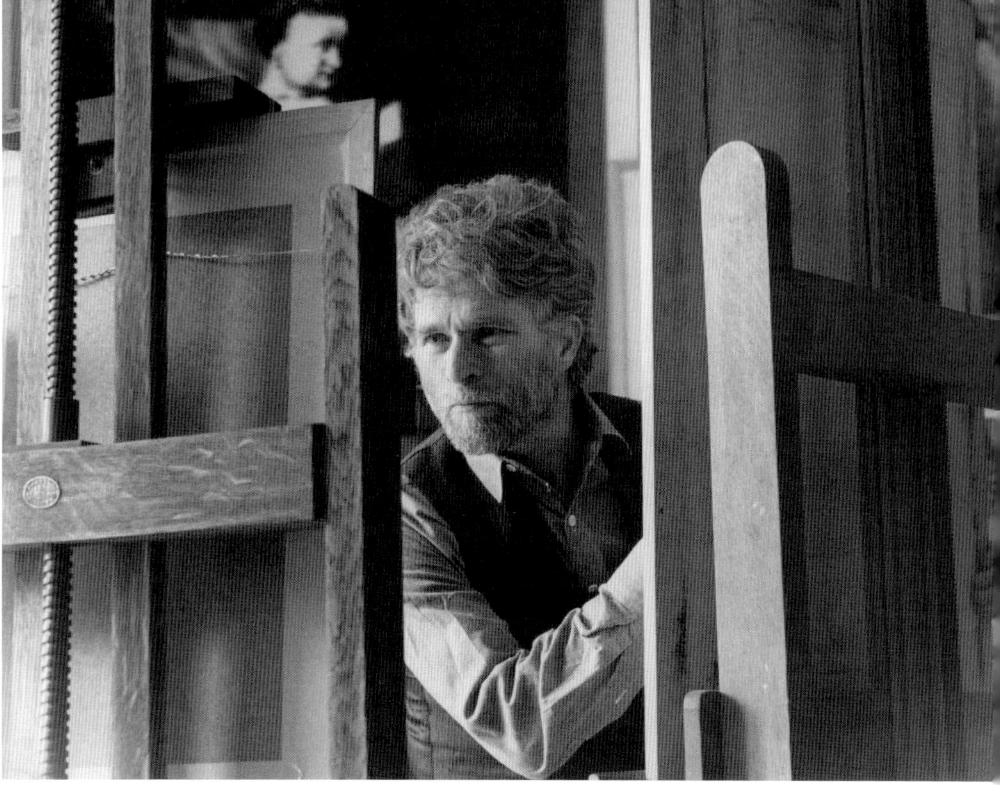

Kitaj in his studio, April 1980.

1 FEBRUARY 1980
A CONVERSATION.

MJ. RB telephoned.

He said the picture was going well. Said Sandra had come in one evening when he was exasperated with my face and he asked her to figure it out. He says she "discovered some proportions" which are just right (for the painting) and also look like me. Working from photos, etc.. He said it was marvellous—first time he's ever worked with anyone that way. It will be painted over, but he's photographed the drawing for us.

10 FEBRUARY 1980

MJ. It's now started to have layers of splodges over the base colours. "Yes", says RB, "It will never be finished—just layered." SJ had been done in colours over the blue. The drawing of my head was there in profile in charcoal. He said he's happy with some bits but not others—he's been working on it only in afternoons with models coming every morning.

He had me stand with one leg in front of the other and one hand on a pile of books—very unnatural—and drew a new body outline with the blue paint. Said he wouldn't do my shirt Yale blue—doesn't go with other things especially the van Gogh colours. But wants no collar—long neck. Made me rumple up my shirt a bit so it wouldn't cover my bottom. He did the new outline, with two possibilities for the front of the torso—about 3/4" apart, depending on the composition. He said he thought the body for the first time had life (?) in the composition (see overleaf).

Then he worked on the head—this time brushing on hair colour with a brush, and then mixing flesh colour—and painting some arm and face. He said "you look like something from Picasso's blue period", and ended, as usual, with the turpentine bottle out, rubbing the colour off my nose. I'm not wild about it—sinuous caricature of a neck with a head like an acorn perched on top.*

Harry identified everyone in the painting except me—said it was RB.

* note by Sandy: RB said the neck was a reference to Piero della Francesca (?from the Sheba Solomon painting?)

Opposite and overleaf: Photographs of work in progress, RB Kitaj.

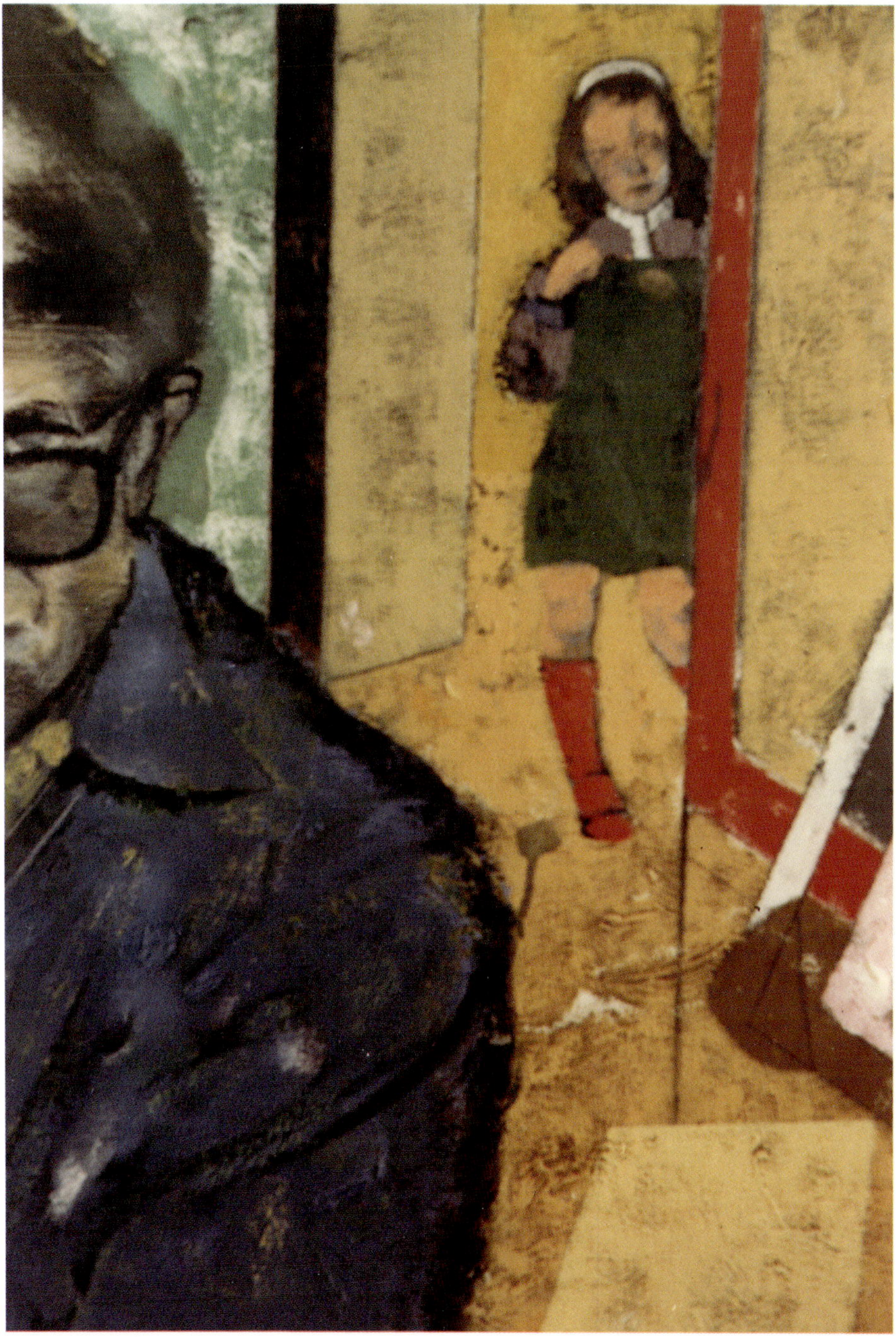

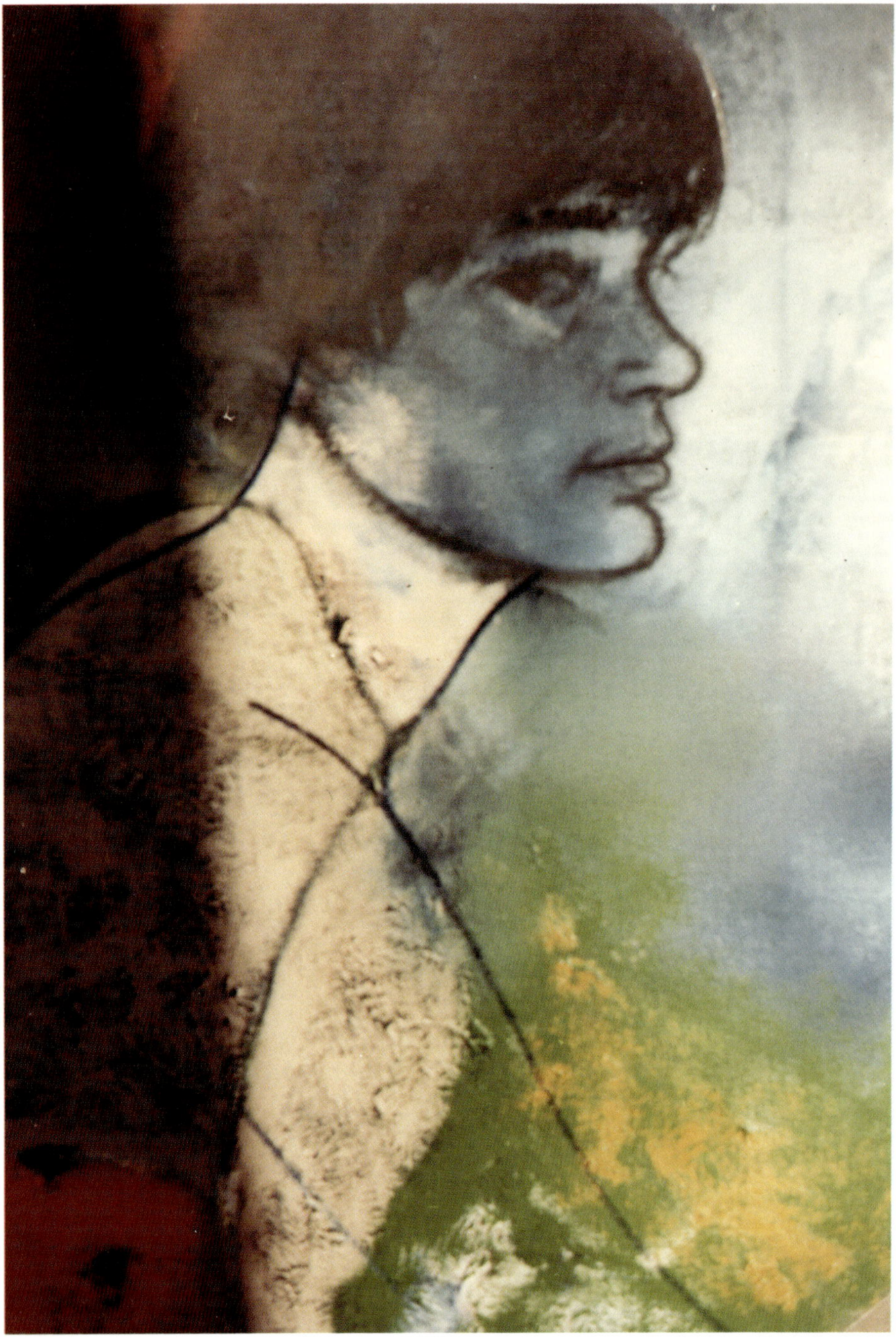

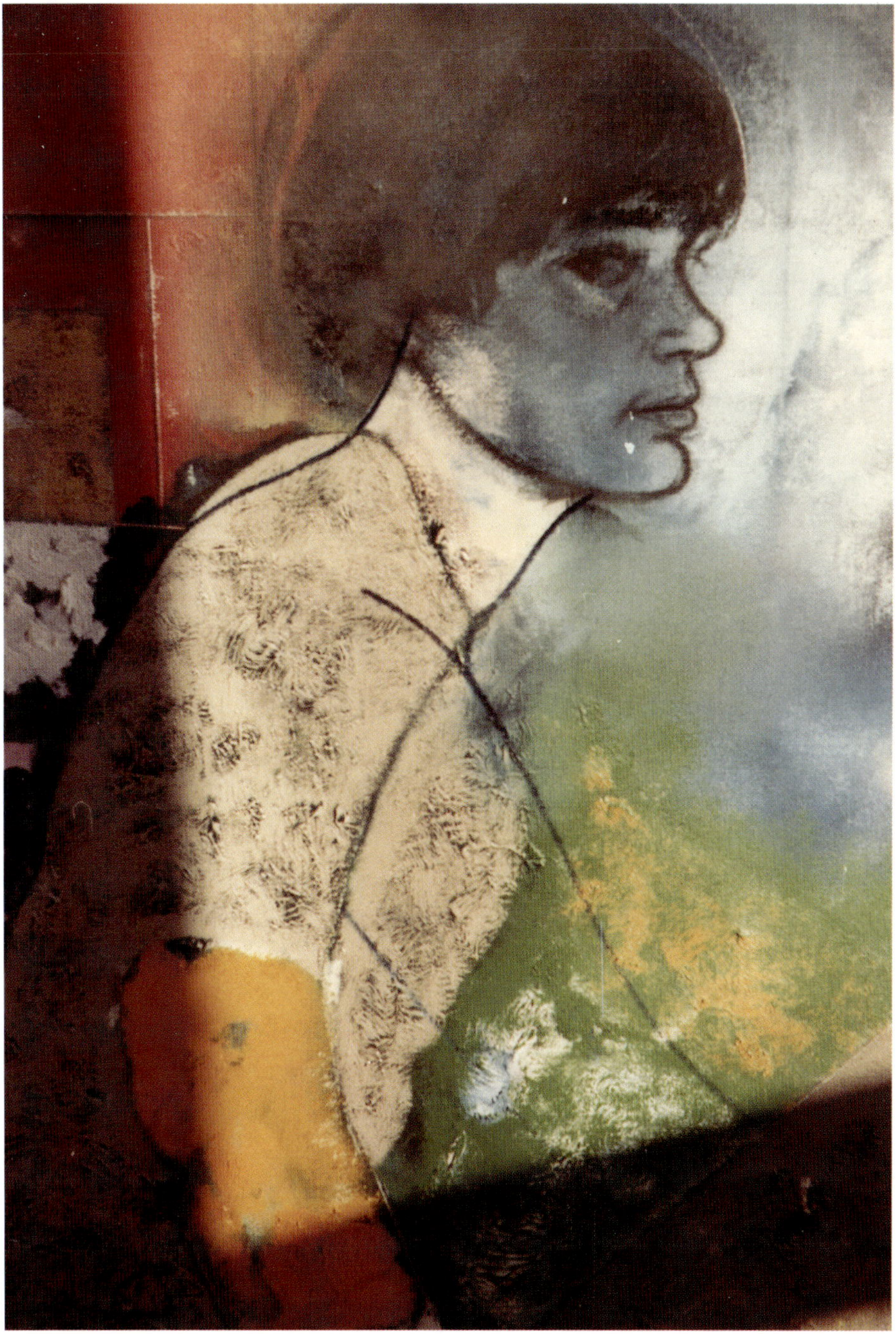

23 FEBRUARY 1980 (SATURDAY)

SANDY. (From memory ten days later)

We were both indulging in general anti-social crustiness; RB slightly penitent about refusing to do an Ellsworth Kelly party at Suzy Gablik. "I just can't bear to meet new people. It just seems to get more difficult as you grow older." So I quoted David Roberts' story about Eliot's response at High Table to the small talk—"You must find after so long that it comes easy to you to write", to which Eliot said "No, the older you get the more you know and the more difficult it is to write." RB picks down *Little Gidding* from the shelf and slowly spat out the passage "Let me disclose the gifts reserved for age.... The cold friction of expiring sense... the conscious impotence of rage... the rending pain of re-enactment... the shame of motives late revealed...." That made us feel better and so he painted away at my face. The picture behind my head has been reduced from square to vertical format with the repentir showing ("you can't scrape out impastoed brushwork"). When I likened the composition (I'm referring to the downward thrust of the frame onto my head) to Mantegna's "circumcision" RB immediately took the point; knew the painting.

He seems happier about the painting of MJ—referred to Sandra's two contributions ("David can do that too—tell you exactly what somebody's nose is like..."). I'm not so happy about it.

26 APRIL 1980 (SATURDAY)

SANDY. RBK gets painting out—"Haven't looked at it for ages... been so preoccupied with Dominie" (his daughter), and the suicide, by jumping from Clifton Suspension Bridge, of the girl who has been a model for Sandra and whose friend at St Paul's School is Kitaj's model.

(In the meantime, he has done a lot more work on the painting—books now in the bookcase; a lamp from ceiling top left; MJ's Yale jersey stripes and number now on; Harry's hair; further touches to Sarah Jane more to MJ's face; a cat in the "picture" bottom right).

Let's see.... "It IS interesting, but it is awkward. Manet's compositions were awkward (Alan Bowness wrote well on that 15 years ago); it drove his friends mad and the critics hated him for it. This has these gratuitous injections from the van Gogh and that on top of all our distress over Dominie... strange painting... there are passages which really get me.... Let's work on the face more—I'd like to smooth it out a little—you know I've never painted as thick as this before."

RB had been to dinner with Bacon two nights before—Bacon fulminating against everyone (Auerbach stupid expressionist lines, etc.). Referring to Somerset Maugham's description of himself as "at the front of the second row" he said "that's where I am too, but let me add without arrogance that there isn't anyone in the front row now—not even Bacon or Balthus." I "de Kooning?"—RBK "No, though he's the best painter in the United States—I say that though I wouldn't know how to judge someone like Stella."

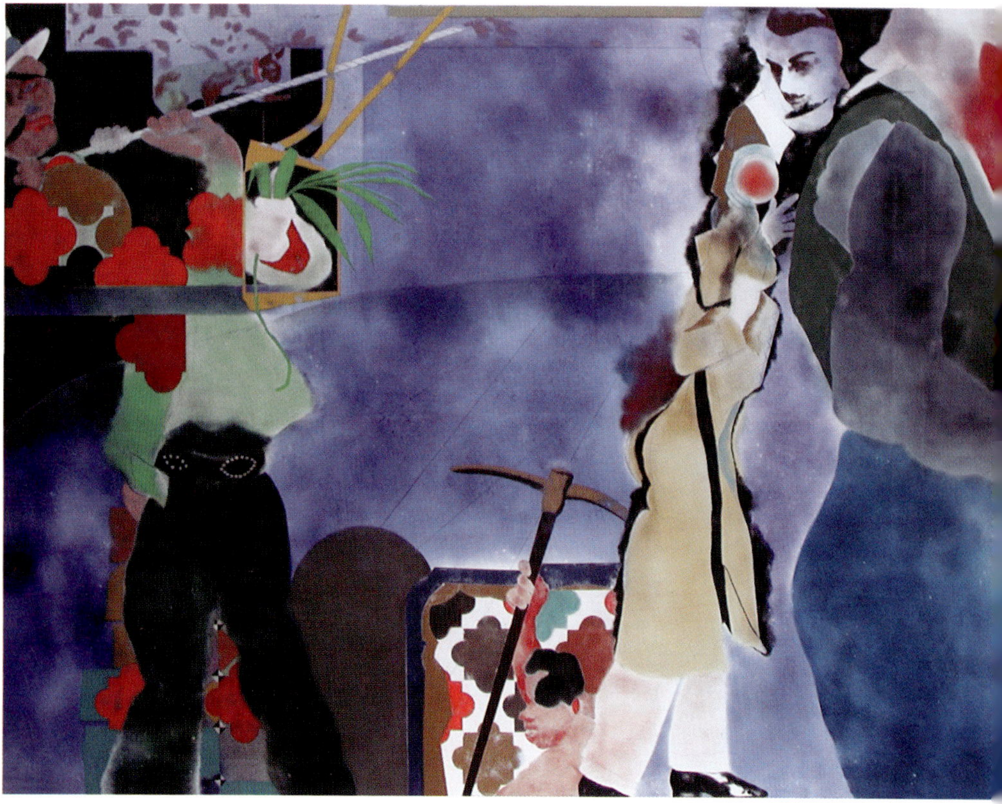

Kitaj paints away very intensely on the face for nearly two hours—virtually no break; very tiring. "Is your face thinner than it was?"... "I've got the nose all wrong."

When he's finished, he doesn't want me to look at it. "Let me know whenever you can come again."

(RBK wants to have the right panel of *Pacific Coast Highway* to do more work on it—it's too 'empty'.)

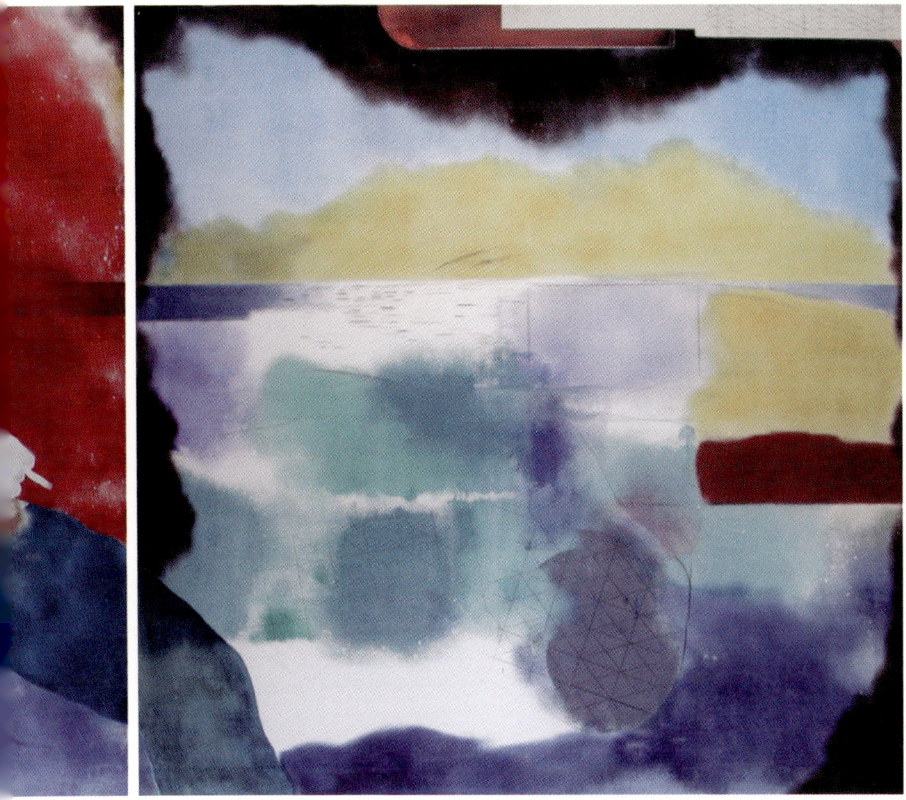

Pacific Coast Highway, RB Kitaj, 1973.

7 JUNE 1980
(SATURDAY)

SANDY. I go at 11:15. It is the day after *The Spectator* article by Gavin Stamp attacking me and I am still stunned by the venom of it.

RB gets out the painting, sucks his teeth, hasn't seen it for weeks and hums away happily. He has done a great deal to simplify it by a massive over painting in red (not only over all the books but down behind me—the 'picture halo' has gone from behind my head) and this has greatly unified the surface that had previously been very fragmented in its patterning and range of colours. He mumbled approval of my blue shirt and above all the interlocking of fawn shapes around MJ. He relishes the 'awkwardness' of the composition. (This is characteristic in Manet's work that he likes so much.) He referred to the difficulty he has in (I think I remember this correctly) reconciling the problems of light falling from a certain direction and the demands of the picture as a composition: he wants to take better photographs of both me and MJ and intends to do most of the rest of the work NOT working from the model. (Note: John Golding and James Joll told me that they had no sittings at all for the painting of them.)

All the same, he worked hard redrawing me (then we had lunch). And then a further hour or so of drawing and photographs.

He had hoped to get the painting done to submit to an exhibition (in Southampton?) of modern portraits (like the Portrait Gallery show) of famous people (!).

He gave me the pencil drawing of MJ's and my head as a consolation prize for the delay—saying that someone had said it looked like a Dürer—but that he wouldn't exactly want us to hang it on the wall! (I look like a ratty Stanley Spencer and MJ has only one eye.)

My eyes ache like hell since I am glaring (out of focus) over the top of my specs.

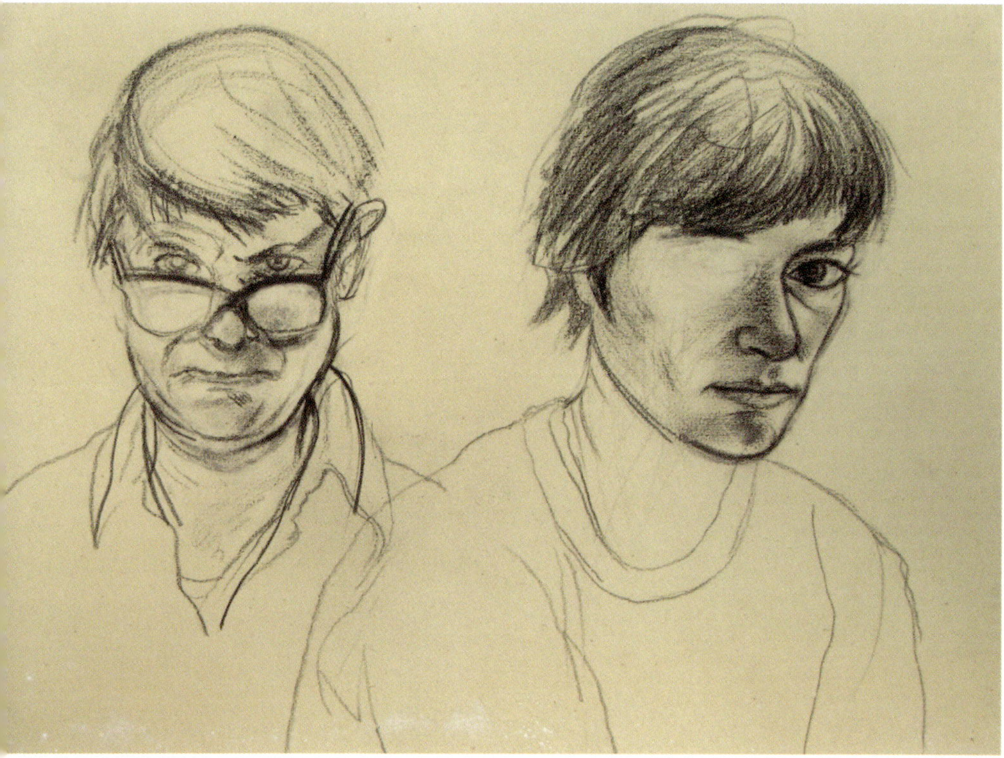

Sketch, RB Kitaj.

19 FEBRUARY 1981

SANDY. I have lunch at the Chinese restaurant with RB. He's just back from Rome—ecstatic about it and some further blossoming in his relations with Sandra. RB morose about state of criticism in London. He had almost put down a deposit on a house next to David H, in Los Angeles. Now would like to spend six months of the year in Rome. *The Last Judgment* changed his life....

He got out the painting, hummed away, pretty pleased with it. Said if he were starting from scratch now it would be very different—more gestural in its brush work: was happier now that the colour was more coordinated and related to the van Gogh pool room reproduction.

He repainted the lower half of my face and seemed very pleased with it. Talked about David Hockney as usual—"the boy's a genius". I said I don't believe in his world. RB: "I don't either but all the same he shares with Hopper and Sickert the position of being unique in this century in pinning down the real qualities of a place." Me: "But I don't like California either." RB: "Me too... but all the same he's a genius."

I find it impossible to judge the painting (though it is odd to look at my face since I am now doing a self-portrait—my first painting in 30 years), since I so much had hoped for something in the manner of his John Golding/James Joll or at least Orientalist manner.

Sandra returned. We talked of Rome, Borromini and David Sylvester's passion for the courtyard of Santa Maria della Pace (I explain about the corner column order) and then Avigdor Arika's wife arrived and over tea we talked of modern Hebrew literature (I recalling the discussion at InterFaculty "A" (Cambridge Committee) of yesterday in which someone had asked about the worthwhileness of recent Hebrew literature as a subject of study) and I was told the story about the crowd who finished the last line when Pasternak forgot the words.

The painting was transferred from Elm Park Road to Grove End Road on 18 November 1981. Mrs Bennett in charge while MJ away at Yale.

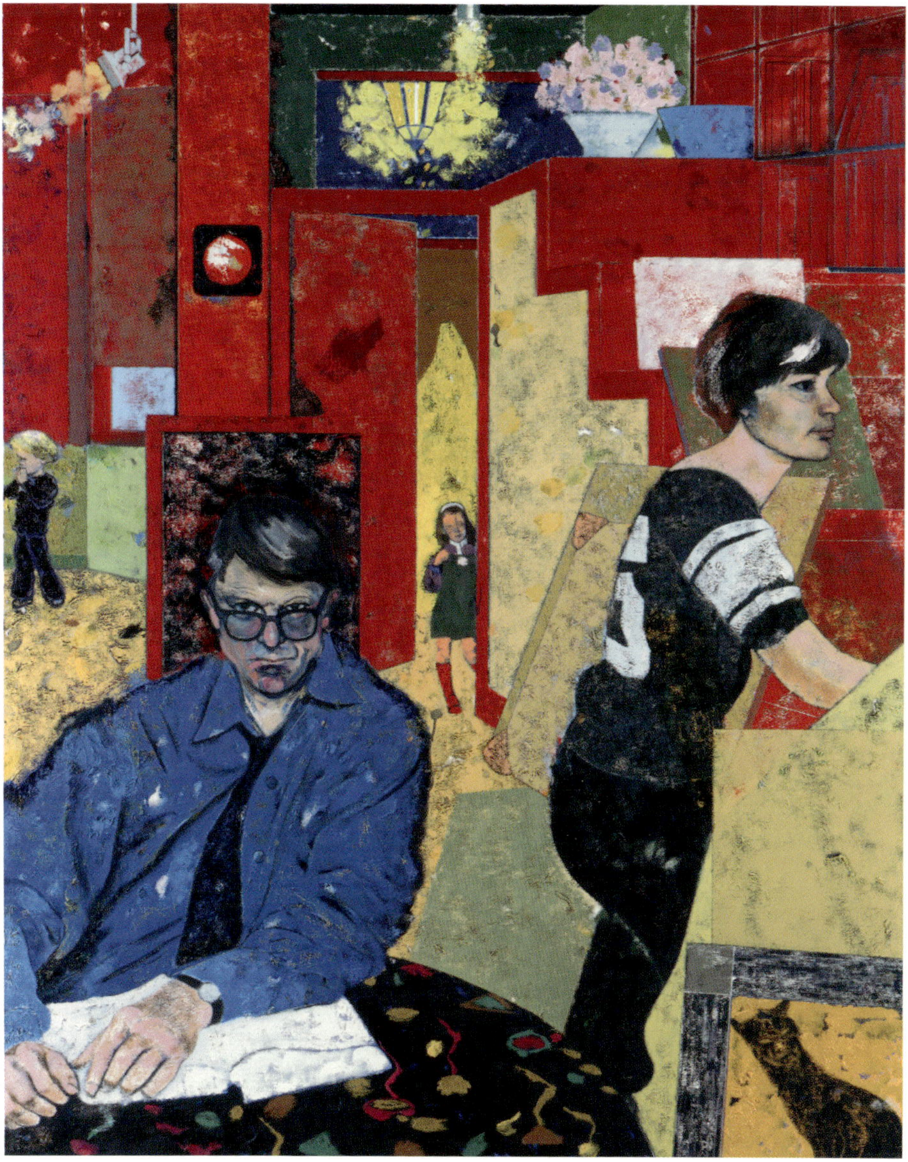

The finished painting: *The Architects*, RB Kitaj, 1981, private collection.

27 NOVEMBER 1981

SANDY. On MJ's return we planned a celebration dinner. RB and Sandra came on Friday night (MJ's mum due to fly in the following morning).

We started with avocado dip and fritos and drank to the painting (Kitaj in grape juice). Then chicken tetrazzini and thick brown bread—RBK had three helpings—and Mrs Bennett's apple crumble. RBK says "That's the best meal I've had in years." MJ says "RB you're the one guest that makes all this damn cooking into a pleasure".

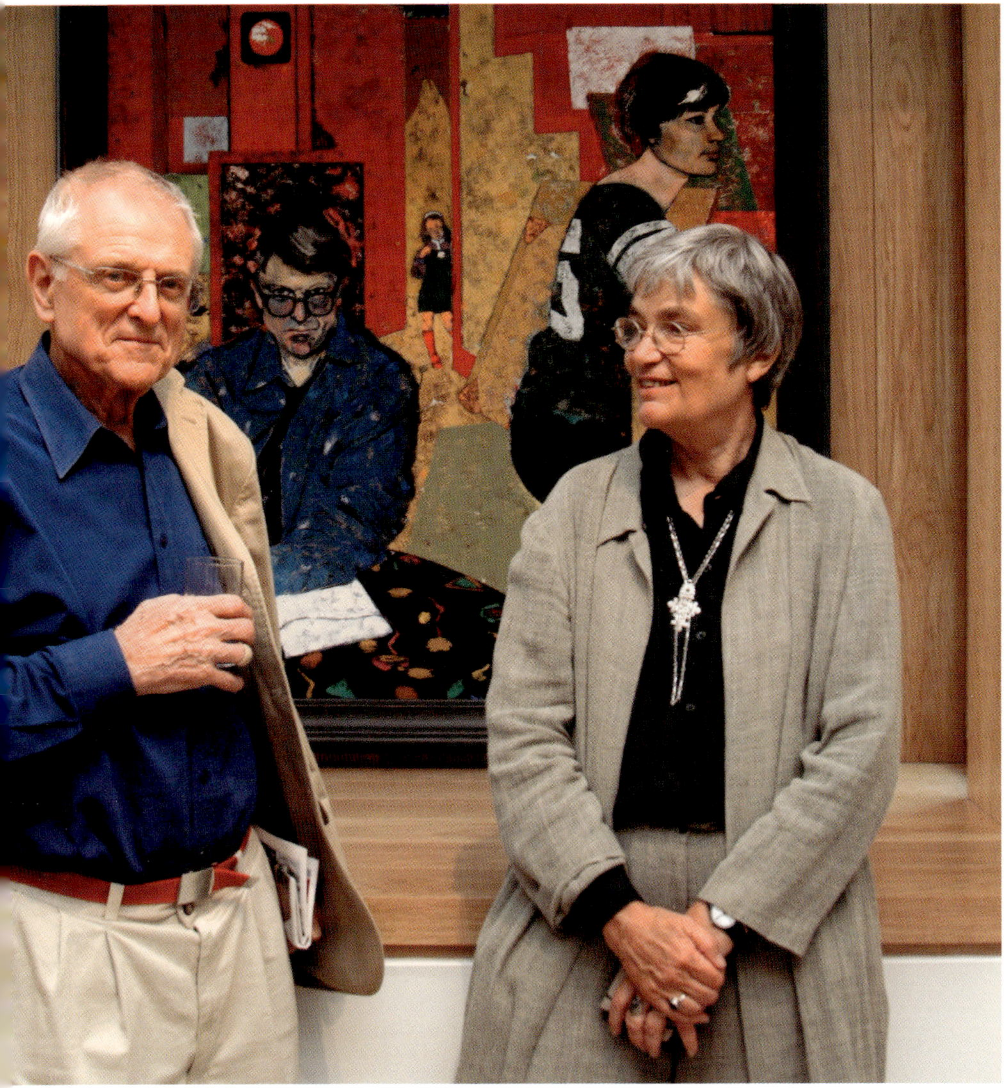

Sandy, MJ, and *The Architects* at the opening of Pallant House, July 2006.

PICTURE CREDITS

Courtesy Marlborough Fine Art and Kitaj estate	cover image, p 4, p 43
Peter Cook	p 8, p 27
John Donat / RIBA Photographic Library	p 6, p 11, p 26
Yale University Art Gallery: Bequest of Stephen Carlton Clark, BA 1903	p 13
RB Kitaj (all progress photos)	pp 14–15, pp 17–22, p 25, pp 33–35
Permission from the National Gallery / Marlborough Fine Art and Kitaj estate	p 29, p 30
Raven Smith	pp 38–39
Anne-Katrin Purkiss	p 45

ACKNOWLEDEGMENTS

Thanks to Geoffrey Partar of Marlborough Fine Art,
and to the estate of RB Kitaj.

Dedication: to Lem, Dominie, and Max.

Designed by Rachel Pfleger @ bdp

Black Dog Publishing Limited / 10A Acton Street / London / WC1X 9NG
E. info@blackdogonline.com / W. www.blackdogonline.com

British Library Cataloguing-in-Publication Data.
A CIP record for this book is available from the British Library.

ISBN 978 1 906155 44 5

Black Dog Publishing is an environmentally responsible company.
Kitaj: The Architects is printed on Lumisilk, paper with ECT fibre sourced from well managed and sustainable forests, from ISO 14001 and ISO 9001 accredited supplier, and on Cairn Multi Kraft, a 100% recycled paper.

reuse recycle reduce

architecture art design
fashion history photography
theory and things

www.blackdogonline.com

black dog publishing
london uk